SCRIBE PUBLICATIONS

BEST OF BRITAIN'S POLITICAL CARTOONS 2013

Dr Tim Benson is Britain's leading authority on political cartoons. He runs *The Political Cartoon Gallery*, the world's largest website for the sale of original cartoon art, and regularly curates exhibitions at his Cartoon Café in Eastbourne, UK. He has produced numerous books on political cartoonists, including *Churchill in Caricature*, *Low and the Dictators*, *The Cartoon Century: modern Britain through the eyes of its cartoonists*, and *Drawing the Curtain: the Cold War in cartoons*.

BEST OF BRITAIN'S POLITICAL CARTOONS 2013

EDITED BY TIM BENSON

SCRIBE
Melbourne • London

Scribe Publications Pty Ltd

18–20 Edward St, Brunswick, Victoria 3056, Australia
50A Kingsway Place, Sans Walk, London, EC1R 0LU, United Kingdom

First published by Scribe 2013

Cover image credit: Peter Brookes
Cover image design: Scribe Publications

Printed and bound in England by CPI Group (UK) Ltd

National Library of Australia
Cataloguing-in-Publication data

Benson, Tim, editor.
The Best of Britain's Political Cartoons 2013

9781922247049 (UK Paperback)

1. Political cartoons. 2. English wit and humor, Pictorial. 3. Great Britain–Politics and
government–Caricatures and cartoons.

320.9410207

scribepublications.com.au
scribepublications.co.uk

CARTOONISTS

INTRODUCTION

'PLUS ÇA CHANGE, plus c'est la même chose,' said a 19th-century French journalist by the name of Jean-Baptiste Alphonse Karr. For those who, like me, did not pass their French O-level, the saying translates as 'The more things change, the more they remain the same.' This could not be truer than in the world of modern British politics. Over the years our political leaders, one after another, have promised us a brighter future while, in reality, the economy has lurched from one crisis to the next. Politicians come and go, but every passing year has its examples of political ineptitude, corruption, scandal, and the proverbial 'passing of the buck'.

Reflect on Sidney Strube's 'Turning 'em Corner' cartoon published on 4 May 1929 (right). With minor alterations to dates and prime ministers, this visual metaphor could easily have been drawn today — nothing changes, does it? The same issues and problems continue to confront us today.

Our political leaders have always promised us better times and a brighter future in their attempts to either obtain or retain office. They always tell us that they will fix the mess caused by the last lot. On the rare occasion that a prime minister miraculously appears to repair the damage caused by his or her predecessor, there is undoubtedly a price to pay in the long term. For example, the last Labour government presided over an unprecedented ten years of economic prosperity, but during this period the

seeds were sown for the beginning of one of the worst recessions to hit this country since the 1930s. Despite every prime minister assuring us that things can only get better, there remains a constant credibility gap between what they say and what they achieve.

In 1945, Labour's first majority government offered a New Jerusalem but left office six years later with rationing still in place and the economy faltering — the price of the British Army fighting an overseas war. Does that sound familiar? When the Conservatives returned to office in 1951 with the slogan 'Set the people free', they did nothing of the sort. They appeased the unions and made no attempt to privatise nationalised industries or dismantle the welfare state. When Harold Macmillan told the country in 1957 that Britons 'never had it so good', the economy was again in decline.

In the 1960s, Harold Wilson said that, under a Labour government, a new Britain would be forged by the white heat of technological revolution. It proved nothing more than meaningless hyperbole. John Major came to office in 1990 saying that he wanted a country at ease with itself. The problem was that his party was not at ease with itself, and this led to its disastrous showing at the 1997 general election. Gordon Brown told the House of Commons that he had brought an end to 'boom and bust'. And finally, our current leader, Prime Minister David Cameron, has continued in this vein of political faux pas, claiming that he and his fellow Etonian cabinet ministers, together with the general public, 'are all in it together'.

Fortunately for us, Britain's finest cartoonists have held these politicians' ludicrous utterances to account over the years, ridiculing them for their hubris and uselessness. This country has an unparalleled cartoon heritage, going back to the father of modern political cartooning, James Gillray. From him, the torch has been successfully passed onto John Tenniel, through to Bernard Partridge, Carruthers Gould, Will Dyson, Poy, David Low, Sidney Strube, Leslie Illingworth, Victor 'Vicky' Weisz, Michael Cummings, and Trog, to today's fine crop of cartoonists. As we can see in this collection, the standard and quality of cartooning in Britain remains as strong and as vibrant as ever — at least we can find some humour in the mess and pain the politicians so regularly put us through.

Until the early 1960s, only the tabloid press published political cartoons. The broadsheets considered them too frivolous an item for a 'serious' newspaper. The exception was *The Manchester Guardian*, which syndicated David Low's *Evening Standard* cartoons from the 1930s onwards. In fact, Low was the first cartoonist to be employed by a broadsheet when he left the *Evening Standard* for *The Manchester Guardian* in 1950. The other broadsheets continued to ignore political cartoons until 1966, when Ken Mahood became *The Times*'s first political cartoonist and Nick Garland, *The Daily Telegraph*'s. Today every broadsheet employs a leading political cartoonist, allocating them a layout that tabloid cartoonists can only dream of.

How things have changed. Until the 1990s, just about every tabloid and London evening newspaper employed a political cartoonist of substance. Now, the *Mirror* no longer carries a political cartoon, and it is ten years since the only London evening paper published one, despite the *Evening Standard* having previously employed such eminent cartoonists as Low, Vicky, JAK, and Blower. Mac at the *Daily Mail* and Paul Thomas at the *Daily Express* are not what would be described as overtly political. Their cartoons are topical and gag-oriented, primarily designed to put a smile on the faces of their readers.

It goes without saying that the tabloid newspapers have a completely different readership from that of the broadsheets. The working practices of both the tabloid and the broadsheet cartoonist are also very different. Both Martin Rowson and Steve Bell of *The Guardian* like to work from home, believing it lessens the chance of any editorial interference. Rowson admits that he and Bell are lucky at *The Guardian* because, in his words:

We get a free hand, basically. Steve is more hardline than I am. He won't consult the editors, just delivers his stuff. I tend to outline my intentions in case there is an obvious clash with the column below. Generally, we operate on a kind of internal self-censoring basis, bearing in mind what our readers will be able to stomach.

In comparison, Peter Brookes prefers to work directly from *The Times*'s offices, as does Christian Adams at *The Daily Telegraph*. Not only do they enjoy the buzz of the newsroom, but also find attending the daily editorial news conferences helpful for choosing the subject matter for their cartoons. Brookes admits he's free to ridicule whomever he wants, and has the independence to ignore the paper's political stance. He feels his job is to hold all politicians to account, regardless of their political standpoint: 'You're in permanent opposition; to my mind there's no such thing as cartoons in praise of, or congratulating. It goes against my nature to want to bolster anyone. You cringe from that sort of thing.'

Tabloid cartoonists do not have nearly as much latitude to express themselves. The tabloid cartoonist is expected to present their editor with a number of roughs to choose from. Occasionally, the editor will make a suggestion. Sometimes, the editor's decision is not made until late in the day, which has ramifications for the cartoonist. As Andy Davey explains further: 'They seem to enjoy the macho brinkmanship of the late decision, just bringing the ship round in time. It makes for frayed nerves, but it may add some energy to my drawing.'

Each new generation of political leaders throws up interesting challenges and opportunities for cartoonists to capture what David Low called their 'inner essence'.

Our political leaders appear to be getting younger and younger, which makes caricature harder, as prominent features tend to develop as people age. Nonetheless, cartoonists are having great fun with the likes of Ed Miliband, Nick Clegg, and George Osborne. The main focus of their attention is, of course, Prime Minister David Cameron, whose smooth and shiny pinkish face is, according to Christian Adams, his most prominent feature:

> The first thing I see when I look at Cameron is his skin. It's so shiny and rosy and posh. His forehead is so waxy there's a permanent starburst off it. And his forehead is huge; really bulbous and not helped by a very high hairline. He has permanently flushed cheeks. He has goggly frog-eyes with bags under them and crow's feet to the sides, a little pointy nose and a tiny lipless mouth. I think he's probably heavier in real life than he looks, so I give him chubby jowls.

Like Adams, Steve Bell has concentrated on Cameron's smooth and shiny skin, but his depiction has been contentious, as he continually draws the prime minister with a condom over his head. Bell says he got the idea after noticing how remarkably smooth and taut Cameron's skin was, as if his head had been encased in tight rubber. There was some initial opposition from Bell's editor at *The Guardian*, Alan Rusbridger, who forbade him to depict the prime minister in this way. However, Rusbridger gave Bell the green light when he found his advertisers did not have a problem with it. Cameron has certainly been irked by Bell's depiction of him, recently saying to the cartoonist, 'You can only push the condom so far!'

Martin Rowson and Peter Brookes have both focused more on Cameron's upper-class background. Rowson has had great success by depicting him as Little Lord Fauntleroy, while Brookes constantly associates him with his public-school education at Eton and at Oxford. As Cameron tries his very best to downplay his class, such depictions of him are not appreciated, as Brookes explains: 'Cameron is very touchy about that aspect of things. He doesn't like the idea of the Bullingdon sort of thing being brought up again. I know I get a lot of complaints, which makes me want to do it more.'

To their credit, the cartoonists have been equally cruel with their depiction of the leader of the opposition. Ed Miliband's geekiness, deep-set eyes, and nasal utterances are a gift. Because of his eyes, both Christian Adams and Steve Bell have drawn him as a panda bear. Bell, in particular, has focused all his energies on his eyes: 'I've drawn Ed a few times and he has crazy, staring eyeballs. His brother, David, has similar eyes but nowhere near as dramatic. I once had Gordon Brown tell Ed: "Since Tony left, this government has had a mad-eye deficiency, and you've not one but two."'

Peter Brookes draws Miliband as the cartoon character Wallace from Nick Park's *Wallace and Gromit*. Miliband has even admitted that he does physically resemble Wallace: 'If spin doctors could design a politician,' said Milliband, 'I suspect he wouldn't look like me.' Brookes believes that the comparison with Wallace has damaged Miliband's chances of ever becoming prime minister. This is because, like Wallace, Miliband also appears hapless, making the public's perception of him unsuitable prime-ministerial material.

The cartoonists portray Chancellor of the Exchequer George Osborne as a sinister figure, along with his prominent 'bum' nose. Martin Rowson believes that Osborne's persona is that of a 'public-school bully with a permanent cocky sneer'. Christian Adams sees Osborne as

the pantomime villain straight from central casting. That grey bloodless skin. Those dark eyes (I even add some blue to the flesh colour), that sneering sideways mouth, his dark hair, which I make jet black and greasy, and best of all, his wonderful nose. I got a letter from a reader outraged that I give him a "penile, testicular nose" and I thought, *Good!* I've seen him in real life and he's actually very unremarkable, so thank goodness he photographs like this.

Steve Bell has a genius for the surreal and pushing the boundaries of taste to its limit. He constantly shows Osborne in a gimp mask and bondage gear. This, I imagine, is a reference to Osborne's earlier friendship with Natalie Rowe, a dominatrix who called herself Miss Whiplash. According to Rowe, Osborne was fascinated by her world of whips, chains, and rubber bondage equipment. When interviewed, Bell states that his depiction of Osborne is more to do with the chancellor's determination to cut the national debt. According to Bell, 'The whole point about George's stance is it's about restraint, restraint, restraint, cuts, cuts, whips, whips, straps, straps, chains, chains.'

Deputy Prime Minister Nick Clegg has proved somewhat more difficult to caricature, mainly because of his blandness and lack of prominent features. Christian Adams believes this is because 'he does actually look like a cardigan-catalogue male model'. Steve Bell concurs that Clegg lacks substance: 'Clegg is so blank, which is always going to be a problem for a young politician. There are no salient features you can grab and hang on to.'

As a consequence, Bell invariably draws him as a cardboard cut-out, metaphorically similar to Rowson's depiction of Clegg as Pinocchio. Despite being deputy prime minister and leader of the Liberal Democrats, the perception is that he has no power or authority and is a prisoner of the Tories. This is the way Peter Brookes depicts him, in the guise of Cameron's Etonian fag and lackey 'Cleggers'. According to Brookes:

> Clegg is very much the junior partner, while Cameron has that air of entitlement about him. So the idea of Cameron as a prefect and Clegg as his fag seemed a theme that is infinitely playable. I've called him 'Cleggers' because it's a public-school way of addressing somebody. The Lib Dems are a party to the left of Labour and they are doing the Tories' bidding — they are fig leaves, being used to justify Tory policy.

> At Prime Minister's Question Time, you can see Clegg immediately behind Cameron. You can tell he's uncomfortable, as you would be if you were having all this stuff heaped upon you by the Tories. The whole thing is riddled with these wonderful, strange anomalies that will never be resolved, which is why the Coalition is so good for cartoonists.

Like Brookes, Chris Riddell of *The Observer* does not find Clegg's blandness a drawback. According to Riddell:

> The reason Clegg is such a gift to draw is certainly not to do with his physical appearance; he's a pretty ordinary-looking bloke. He doesn't have glasses, doesn't have a beard, he's not balding … But his political position makes him an absolute gift, because of his status in this

Coalition. So week after week, we do Clegg as a lapdog, a ventriloquist's dummy … Little Clegg Riding Hood, with the Tory wolf waiting in the woods.

The last year has seen Tory backbenchers rebelling over Europe, a prime minister kowtowing to an American president, MPs and Lords accepting cash for questions, British troops fighting and dying abroad, a prime minister wanting to meddle in the Middle East, scandals at the BBC and in the Health Service, and a struggling British economy, with both the government and the opposition blaming each other for the mess. And, to top it all, just as I have completed this anthology for 2013, the Chancellor of the Exchequer, George Osborne popped up and informed us that 'we have turned the corner' (as depicted below by Steve Bell). You could not make it up!

I wonder if someone picking up this book in ten years' time, when we'll have a new generation of politicians in charge, will think, 'Not much has changed, has it?'

"BRITAIN IS TURNING A CORNER"

THE CARTOONS

Patrick Blower
The Daily Telegraph
3 August 2012

Fresh from cheering a Russian judo star on to a gold medal at the Olympic Games, President Vladimir Putin urged leniency for members of a female punk band, Pussy Riot, on trial for protesting against him at the altar of a Moscow cathedral. However, since returning to the Russian presidency in May, Putin had instigated a crackdown on political dissenters.

'A curse of Bradley Wiggins!'

Mac
Daily Mail
3 August 2012

Bradley Wiggins claimed a British-record seventh Olympic medal with a sensational gold in the men's time trial. Wiggins's high-profile success in the Tour de France and the London Olympics translated into a renewed enthusiasm for cycling in Britain.

Chris Riddell
The Observer
5 August 2012

President Assad's bloody defiance risked wider conflict in the Middle East. Lebanon had asked Syria to avoid incursions by its troops into Lebanese territory as several Lebanese civilians, including women and children, had been killed during border skirmishes.

Steve Bell
The Guardian
7 August 2012

Nick Clegg's plan for constitutional reform lay in ruins as David Cameron was unable to persuade Tory backbenchers to support an elected House of Lords. The announcement represented a personal blow to Clegg, who had championed wide-scale political reform as a distinctive Liberal Democrat contribution to the coalition. It left Clegg increasingly reliant on an upturn in the economy, progress on social mobility, and a broader liberal agenda to justify the original decision to form the coalition with Cameron.

Brighty
The Sun
6 August 2012

London Mayor Boris Johnson made his presence felt at the Olympic Games when he was left dangling six metres in the air after getting stuck on a zip wire. Johnson claimed his rocketing popularity would 'all come crashing down' after the Olympics while brushing aside polls that put him as favourite to succeed David Cameron as Tory leader. Cameron joked later that only Johnson could get away so well with getting stuck on a wire. 'If any other politician anywhere in the world was stuck on a zip wire it would be a disaster. For Boris, it's an absolute triumph.'

Steve Bell
The Guardian
8 August 2012

The prime minister abandoned Lib Dem plans for reforming the House of Lords because of strong opposition from his own party. Changes to the make-up of the Lords would have seen 80 per cent of peers elected and the total number of members halved to 450. Despite this, Cameron defiantly refused to drop plans to reduce the size of the House of Commons: 'We should have a House of Commons that is smaller, less expensive, and we should have equal-sized seats,' he said.

Martin Rowson
Morning Star
8 August 2012

There was widespread criticism of the corporate-sponsorship takeover of the Olympic Games. Health campaigners also demanded that the International Olympic Committee ban junk-food and fizzy-drink brands from future sporting sponsorship deals, stating that the committee had squandered the chance to create a positive health legacy from the 2012 games.

SLOWER, LOWER, WEAKER

Ingram Pinn
The Financial Times
11 August 2012

Sir Mervyn King, governor of the Bank of England, warned that the impact of the Olympics would not be long-lasting on the economy, but he did say there were lessons to be learnt for the banking sector from the 'fair play' of the games. 'The games have made us all feel better ... but ultimately the games cannot alter the underlying economic situation we face,' King said.

Peter Schrank
The Independent
on Sunday
13 August 2012

More than 20 schools were to lose their playing fields after it emerged the government had approved the sell-off of the green spaces despite pledging an Olympic legacy for children. The news of the sell-off contradicted a pledge by the Coalition to protect school playing fields.

WIKIMMUNITY

Ingram Pinn
The Financial Times
18 August 2012

The Foreign Secretary, William Hague, stated that Britain 'remains committed' to its obligation to extradite Julian Assange to Sweden despite his being granted political asylum by Ecuador. Britain did not recognise Assange's asylum status, he added.

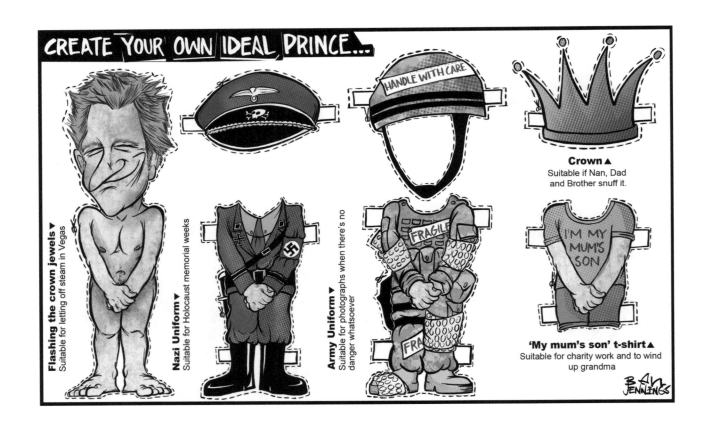

Ben Jennings
i
25 August 2012

The Sun became the first British newspaper to publish photographs of Prince Harry naked in a Las Vegas hotel room, claiming the move was in the public interest. One of the two naked pictures of Harry was splashed across the paper's front page with the headline 'Heir it is!', a day after a male reporter and a female intern posed in a mock-up.

Christian Adams
The Daily Telegraph
29 August 2012

Tim Yeo, a former environment minister, believed that David Cameron should push ahead with a third runway at Heathrow. 'The prime minister must ask himself whether he is man or mouse. Does he want to be another Harold Macmillan, presiding over a dignified slide towards insignificance, or is there, somewhere inside his heart, an organ that still remains impenetrable to most Britons, a trace of Thatcher, determined to reverse the direction of our ship?'

Martin Rowson
The Guardian
1 September 2012

Squatting was to become a criminal offence in England and Wales, punishable by up to six months in jail and fines up to £5000.

Chris Riddell
The Observer
9 September 2012

In an impassioned speech that rocked the Democratic Convention, former president Bill Clinton proclaimed, 'I know we're coming back' from the worst economic mess in generations, and appealed to Americans to support Obama for a second term. To the cheers of thousands of Democrats packed into the convention hall, Clinton said that things were indeed getting better, 'and if you'll renew the president's contract you will feel it'.

Steve Bell
The Guardian
6 September 2012

The prime minister and the chancellor planned to kickstart the economy by lifting planning-permission requirements. The government signalled plans for a major deregulation of planning laws, raising the prospect of allowing more development of green-belt land. The announcement of new legislation, which the government hoped would be 'fast-tracked' into law by October, was also seen as an acknowledgement that the economy needed a major injection of capital.

Peter Schrank
*The Independent
on Sunday*
9 September 2012

President Obama accepted his party's nomination at the Democratic Convention and acknowledged that times were tough: 'The first time I addressed this convention in 2004, I was a younger man; a Senate candidate from Illinois who spoke about hope, not blind optimism or wishful thinking, but hope in the face of difficulty; hope in the face of uncertainty; that dogged faith in the future which has pushed this nation forward, even when the odds are great; even when the road is long.'

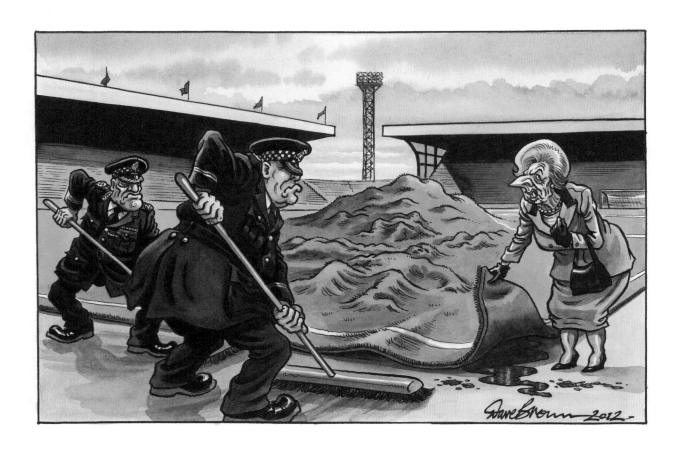

Dave Brown
The Independent
13 September 2012

The independent inquiry into the Hillsborough tragedy detailed the huge scale of the police cover-up, and the willingness of Margaret Thatcher's government to accept it at face value. According to the cartoonist, this cartoon attracted some criticism for being in bad taste, but the correspondence from Liverpool fans was unanimously favourable.

Steve Bell
The Guardian
19 September 2012

On 13 September, a French magazine had published photographs of the Duchess of Cambridge sunbathing topless while on holiday at the Château d'Autet in the south of France. The royal couple laid a criminal complaint to the French Prosecution Department. The next day, the courts granted an injunction against the magazine prohibiting further publication of the pictures.

Bob Moran
The Daily Telegraph
21 September 2012

According to the cartoonist: 'Nick Clegg's YouTube video in which he apologised for breaking his pledge about tuition fees was, in itself, hilarious. I was a bit stuck for how to respond to it, but thought a funny next step would be a further video in which he said sorry for saying sorry. This one got a mention on Radio 2's breakfast show.'

Morten Morland
The Times
24 September 2012

Gales swept in from the English Channel battering the Lib Dem Conference in Brighton. A new poll recorded a swing against the Lib Dems which would, with Clegg remaining at the helm, probably halve the size of their parliamentary party if a general election were held.

THE GATE ESCAPE

Christian Adams
The Daily Telegraph
25 September 2012

Government Chief Whip Andrew Mitchell, who was leaving No. 10 by bicycle, swore at a police officer who told him to exit through the pedestrian gate rather than by the main gate. The leaked official police log of the incident stated that Mitchell said, 'Best you learn your fucking place. You don't run this fucking government ... You're fucking plebs.' In response to the allegations, Mitchell apologised, but disputed many of the details of the accusations, in particular that he had used the word 'pleb'.

FINAL STAGE

2ⁿᵈ STAGE

1ˢᵗ STAGE

90%

70%

RED LINE

Ingram Pinn
The Financial Times
29 September 2012

At the UN General Assembly, Israeli Prime Minister Benjamin Netanyahu drew his 'red line' for Iran's nuclear program despite an American refusal to set an ultimatum. He said Tehran would be on the brink of building a nuclear weapon in less than a year. Holding up a cartoon-like drawing of a bomb with a fuse, Netanyahu literally drew a red line just below a label reading 'final stage', in which Iran was 90 per cent along the path of having sufficient weapons-grade material.

Patrick Blower
The Daily Telegraph
29 September 2012

Ed Miliband and Ed Balls insisted their working relationship was not turning into a repeat of Tony Blair and Gordon Brown's. The pair used separate interviews to reject reports from the shadow cabinet that they were struggling to get on. The tenth series of *Strictly Come Dancing* had just begun on BBC1.

Christian Adams
The Daily Telegraph
30 September 2012

The prime minister said Britain should plough ahead with its 'own agenda' as Europe began a period of dramatic change following the eurozone crisis. He insisted the future should see 'less Europe, not more Europe'. The 39th Ryder Cup was being held at the Medinah Country Club in Illinois.

Morten Morland
The Times
1 October 2012

At the Labour Party Conference, Ed Miliband pledged to deliver a brighter future for young people. Miliband also gave the outlines of his radical course, challenging cartels, overhauling the banks, limiting price rises of the private monopolies, and revising the Coalition's expensive and chaotic reforms of the NHS.

Dave Brown
The Independent
1 October 2012

A number of opinion polls concluded that Ed Miliband was not being perceived as prime ministerial by the electorate and was less popular and less able than David Cameron. According to the cartoonist, 'like the desert-island castaway, the alien demanding to be taken to "your leader" is a gag-cartoon staple, so it was fun to come up with a new political take on it. I always enjoy drawing strange, unearthly, bug-eyed creatures … and the little green man was fun to draw too.'

Morten Morland
The Times
8 October 2012

The prime minister was overshadowed and upstaged by Boris Johnson at the Conservative Party Conference. A poll in *The Observer* newspaper had given Boris a net plus-30 rating, compared to minus-21 for Cameron. Cameron, however, said he did not feel threatened: 'I think it is great that we have got someone with rock-star status in the Tory Party.'

SPREAD A LITTLE PRIVILEGE AS YOU GO BY; PLEASE TRY...

APOLOGIES TO GUSTAVE DORÉ – – ©Steve Bell 2012 – 3402 · 12·10·12· belltoons.co.uk

Steve Bell
The Guardian
12 October 2012

David Cameron told Conservatives at their party conference he wanted everyone to have the same education he enjoyed at Eton: 'I'm not here to defend privilege, I'm here to spread it.'

Patrick Blower
The Daily Telegraph
13 October 2012

Applause and derision greeted the news that the European Union had won the 2012 Nobel Peace Prize, with British Eurosceptics dismissing the award as a 'farce'. The Nobel Committee in Oslo chose to ignore the multiple crises threatening the EU. Instead, it took the longer and bigger view, praising the EU's historical role in promoting reconciliation and peace, and warning its collapse would see an ominous return to 'extremism and nationalism'.

Martin Rowson
The Guardian
14 October 2012

A growing number of high-profile people and institutions were becoming embroiled in the scandal arising from the sexual-abuse allegations against Jimmy Savile.

Dave Brown
The Independent
20 October 2012

BBC director-general George Entwistle claimed ignorance of much of the investigation into sex abuse perpetrated by Jimmy Savile. The House of Commons Select Committee condemned his 'extraordinary lack of curiosity', and many questioned whether he could retain his job. Only in the post for six weeks, another fortnight saw him gone.

Brighty
The Sun
29 October 2012

Lord Patten, as chairman of the BBC Trust, reiterated a public apology over the Savile affair and declared: 'The BBC must tell the truth and face up to the truth about itself, however terrible.'

Chris Riddell
The Observer
4 November 2012

David Cameron faced a fresh rebellion by Conservative MPs who demanded he take a harder line over the European Union budget.

Christian Adams
The Daily Telegraph
4 November 2012

The two most powerful nations in the world, the United States and China, were about to elect their respective leaders. There was a widespread belief in the West that whoever won the American election would be unable to stop the Chinese eclipsing the United States economically.

Brighty
The Sun
5 November 2012

Trailing in the polls, Cameron faced an uncomfortable balancing act on Europe, an issue that has divided his party for decades. He had to try not to alienate his anti-EU backbenchers and see off the threat from UKIP, while keeping the pro-EU Lib Dems on side and avoid wrecking relations with the EU, Britain's biggest trading partner.

Martin Rowson
The Guardian
5 November 2012

President Obama and his Republican challenger, Mitt Romney, appeared to be in a dead heat with just hours to go until election day.

Andy Davey
The Sun
6 November 2012

Hurricane Sandy crushed Mitt Romney's hope of keeping alive any momentum that he had from the debates. According to the cartoonist: 'National emergencies are a great time for a statesman to look, well, statesmanlike; opportunities not available to those not in office. There was a lot of talk in the media, especially the right-wing US media, that Hurricane Sandy was handled well by the Obama team, thereby giving the Obama campaign an unfair lift in the ostensibly delicately balanced presidential race with Romney. There was good evidence that the lift had begun before Sandy, but why let that get in the way of a good narrative.'

Patrick Blower
The Daily Telegraph
10 November 2012

Nick Clegg characterised allegations over the child-abuse scandals on social networks, such as the false claims about Lord McAlpine, as trial by Twitter. Clegg denounced those spreading false allegations of child abuse on the internet, saying they were going to harm the cause of justice for victims.

Morten Morland
The Times
12 November 2012

There was a growing nervousness in Fleet Street that Lord Leveson's long-awaited report would recommend restrictive regulation that would, in effect, muzzle the press.

Ben Jennings

i

17 November 2012

Along with Xi Jinping as supreme leader, a number of other new Chinese leaders were also sworn in as they were elevated to the Politburo and its Standing Committee, the apex of power. With deepening social tensions over corruption, suppression of human rights, and unbridled government power, Xi said: 'Our party faces many severe challenges, and there are also many pressing problems within the party that need to be resolved, particularly corruption.'

The Higher Politics

① ② ③ ④

Martin Rowson18 / Rowson 12   19·11·12

Martin Rowson
The Guardian
19 November 2012

David Cameron hired the hard-hitting and coarse Australian political consultant Lynton Crosby to run the Tories' general election campaign. Crosby has been described as a cross between Alastair Campbell and Crocodile Dundee. He helped John Howard to four election victories, making him the second-longest-serving Australian prime minister, and masterminded Boris Johnson's two victories in the London mayoral election.

Peter Schrank
The Independent on Sunday
18 November 2012

Israel and Hamas brushed aside international calls for restraint by escalating their lethal conflict over Gaza. Palestinian militants launched hundreds of rockets into Israeli territory, targeting Tel Aviv for the first time, while Israel intensified its aerial assaults and sent armoured vehicles rumbling towards the Gaza border for a possible invasion.

Andy Davey
The Sun
22 November 2012

Roberto Di Matteo was sacked by Chelsea after a 3–0 defeat to Juventus, which left the club on the brink of a Champions League exit. Di Matteo had led Chelsea to the Champions League and FA Cup the previous season. According to the cartoonist: 'The rapid turnaround of Chelsea managers under the increasingly imperial Roman Abramovich was becoming a cliche by the time Benitez was appointed as the replacement for sacked Di Matteo. He didn't last long.'

Dave Brown
The Independent
23 November 2012

David Cameron's stance on the EU budget seemed designed to appeal to the Eurosceptics in his party, but it infuriated Herman Van Rompuy and other European leaders. According to the cartoonist, this is an updated version of an old gag (originally involving a cat and cabbages), but, just like the Tories' traditional disarray over Europe, it continues to amuse.

Gary Barker
Tribune
30 November 2012

Secretary of State for Health Jeremy Hunt stated that the NHS reforms the government was introducing would increase accountability and examine the effectiveness of 'Ofsted-style' inspections. The cartoonist states that he sees it as 'privatisation by the back door, which will inevitably rip the heart out of state provision of public healthcare'.

Martin Rowson
The Guardian
1 December 2012

The prime minister rejected the idea of statutory press regulation, believing it would infringe on free speech, and was unconvinced by Lord Leveson's call for a change in the law. Cameron warned that the legislation required to underpin the regulatory body would create a vehicle for politicians in the future to impose regulation and obligations on the press.

Chris Riddell
The Observer
2 December 2012

David Cameron backtracked on his promise to implement Leveson's proposals in full, preferring a system of regulation more favourable to the press.

Brighty
The Sun
3 December 2012

According to the political editor of *The Sun*, Trevor Kavanagh, press victims such as Hugh Grant, Max Mosley, and Steve Coogan, as pictured here, may have won a victory but risked looking like Avengers. Hugh Grant felt the Leveson report had been too mild and was aghast over David Cameron's subsequent refusal to back it.

LONG-RANGE MUSCLE

Ingram Pinn
The Financial Times
15 December 2012

North Korea successfully launched a rocket, an action labelled by the United States, South Korea, and Japan as a test of technology that could one day deliver a nuclear warhead capable of hitting targets as far away as the United States. North Korea is banned from developing missile technology under UN resolutions, although Kim Jong-un is believed to have continued the state's 'military first' programs put in place by his late father, Kim Jong-il.

Chris Riddell
The Observer
16 December 2012

Ed Miliband made his fiercest attack yet against the chancellor's welfare cuts. The Labour leader said the government was hitting people 'they don't meet and whose lives they will never understand'. *The Hobbit* had just opened at cinemas around the UK.

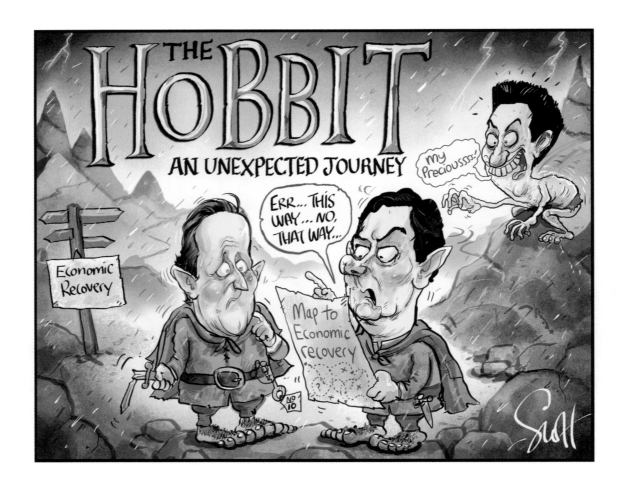

Scott Clissold
Daily Star
16 December 2012

Chancellor George Osborne had admitted the economy was performing less well than expected and the government would miss key debt-reduction targets. Austerity measures were, as a result, extended to 2018. Osborne said 'turning back now would be a disaster' for the UK. Labour responded by saying his credibility was 'in tatters'.

Peter Schrank
The Independent on Sunday
16 December 2012

In May 2013, the government lifted a ban on 'fracking', the controversial drilling technique that has been developed to unlock the gas from shale-rock formations under the ground. 'I would like to see us do more on shale gas,' Osborne told an audience in New York. 'I see with admiration what has happened in the US in the way your shale-gas revolution has made a contribution to GDP.' Fracking had been suspended across the country in 2012 after it was found to have caused two small earthquakes in Lancashire.

Gary Barker
The Times
17 December 2012

Twenty-year-old Adam Lanza fatally shot 20 children and six adult staff members in a mass murder at Sandy Hook Elementary School in Connecticut. Before driving to the school, Lanza had shot and killed his mother, Nancy. The incident was the second-deadliest mass shooting by a single person in American history. The shootings prompted renewed debate about gun control in the United States, as well as a proposal for new legislation banning the sale and manufacture of semi-automatic firearms and magazines with more than ten rounds of ammunition.

Andy Davey
The Sun
19 December 2012

According to the cartoonist: 'The Queen attended a cabinet meeting as part of her Golden Jubilee celebrations, the first monarch to do so since George III in 1781. Well, what would YOU ask Nick Clegg?'

Morten Morland
The Times
22 December 2012

Dense fog caused misery for Christmas holiday travellers at Heathrow and other UK airports. Hundreds of flights were grounded. Heathrow was the worst hit, with 40,000 people affected, and services from Gatwick, Manchester, Glasgow, and Cardiff were also disrupted.

'TIS THE SEASON FOR GIVING

Ingram Pinn
The Financial Times
22 December 2012

Mark Carney left his job as governor of the Bank of Canada to become the new governor of the Bank of England, on an annual salary of £480,000 and pension contributions worth £144,000. On top of that, he receives a £250,000 housing allowance, taking his total package to £874,000. He also receives free health and dental insurance, and the use of a chauffeur-driven car. Consequently, he has become the highest paid central banker in the world, by a significant margin.

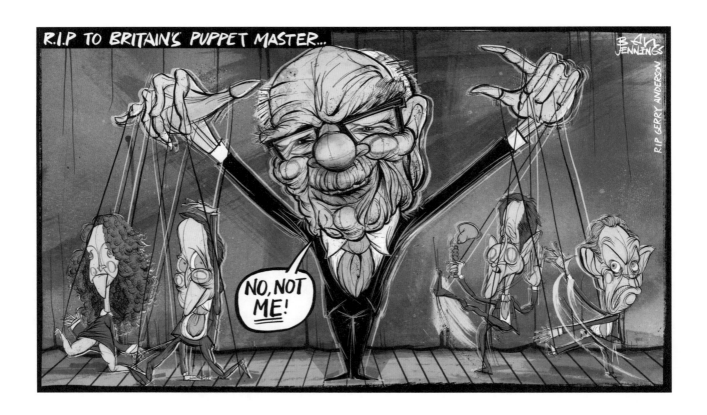

Ben Jennings
i
29 December 2012

The Leveson Inquiry found that Rupert Murdoch was so powerful that he exerted influence over politicians without actually needing to ask them for anything. Leveson said politicians had been competing for Mr Murdoch's support and knew that 'taking him on' would be likely to lead to a backlash from his titles. Gerry Anderson, the creator of hit TV shows including *Thunderbirds*, *Stingray*, and *Joe 90*, died at the age of 83.

Morten Morland
The Times
3 January 2013

President Obama and congressional Republicans faced even bigger budget battles after a hard-fought 'fiscal cliff' deal narrowly averted devastating tax hikes and spending cuts. Republicans, angry the fiscal cliff deal did little to curb the federal deficit, promised to use the debt-ceiling debate to win deep spending cuts next time.

Relaunch!

after Géricault

Martin Rowson
The Guardian
7 January 2013

Cameron and Clegg relaunched the Coalition by making 180 new promises and pledging to work together in the national interest until 2015. In a marked change of tone from the launch of the coalition in May 2010, the prime minister dismissed the idea of a marriage and pledged simply to uphold the two parties' original agreement. Cameron said: 'It is a Ronseal deal. It does what it says on the tin. We said we would come together, we said we would form a government, we said we would tackle these big problems. That is exactly what we have done.'

Andy Davey
The Sun
8 January 2013

Nick Clegg stepped up his efforts to revive his personal approval ratings by agreeing to appear on a weekly phone-in on London's LBC radio station. According to the cartoonist: 'Clegg takes to the airwaves for the first time to face his adoring audience in LBC's weekly "Call Nick Clegg" masochism show. For a man who wants to be loved, he's in the wrong job.'

Peter Brookes
The Times
9 January 2013

The Conservatives forced through cuts in the living standards of the poorest people in the country. Back workers not shirkers, the prime minister declared, as George Osborne pictured an honest shift worker passing the closed blinds of a skiver 'sleeping off a life on benefits'. Tory MP John Redwood insisted betting firms target deprived areas because the poor have too much 'time on their hands'.

Ben Jennings

i

12 January 2013

MPs on all sides of the Commons piled into the Tories, and particularly George Osborne, over the party's developing narrative of 'shirkers vs workers' (or, if you like, 'skivers vs strivers'). Tory MP Sarah Wollaston was one of the first from her side to speak out against the kind of image seen in one of her party's latest campaigns, which depicted an unemployed person slumped on a sofa, apparently unwilling to work.

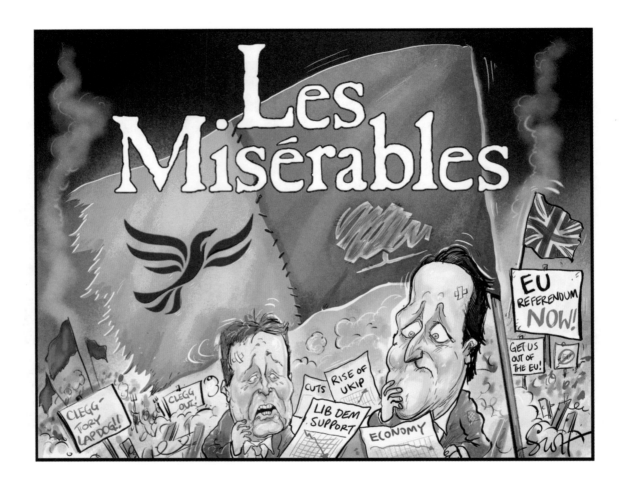

Scott Clissold
Daily Star
13 January 2013   The film *Les Misérables* was released in the UK on 11 January 2013.

'EXTREMELY DISTURBING & COMPLETELY UNACCEPTABLE' DAVID CAMERON

Peter Brookes after 'The Godfather'

Peter Brookes
The Times
17 January 2013

In the House of Commons, David Cameron called for a full investigation into why horsemeat had been found in supermarket beefburgers: 'People in our country would have been very concerned to read this morning that when they thought they were buying beefburgers they were buying something that had horsemeat in it.' Supermarkets had pulled tens of thousands of frozen beefburgers from their shelves after tests had shown that they contained horse and pig DNA.

Patrick Blower
The Daily Telegraph
18 January 2013

High-street retailers HMV, Jessops, and Blockbuster went into receivership due to changes in consumer behaviour. While many high-street shops continue to struggle to meet the cost of rent and business rates, online spending in the UK has more than trebled in the last six years.

Paul Thomas
Daily Express
23 January 2013

More than 5000 soldiers were being axed in a fresh round of defence cuts. Former commanders said the cuts left the army perilously overstretched and unable to take on all the major military commitments demanded by ministers. Under the latest round of redundancies, the army will shrink to 90,000, its lowest level since before the Napoleonic Wars began. Some troops currently on the front line in Afghanistan face the axe next year, the government admitted.

Peter Brookes
The Times
26 January 2013

Nick Clegg, who admitted that the coalition's early cuts on capital spending went too far, said the government would stay the course on its austerity agenda to cut Britain's budget deficit. The deputy prime minister's comments came amid calls for the government to soften austerity as the latest GDP figures released signalled that the UK was lurching towards a triple-dip recession.

Christian Adams
The Daily Telegraph
27 January 2013

Starbucks threatened to suspend millions of pounds of investment in Britain after 'unfair' attacks on its tax affairs by David Cameron. Kris Engskov, the multinational's UK managing director, demanded talks at Downing Street after the prime minister said tax-avoiding companies had to 'wake up and smell the coffee'. Starbucks has found itself under regular attack after it was disclosed that since its arrival in Britain in 1998, it has paid £8.5 million in corporation tax, despite total sales of £3 billion.

Peter Schrank
The Independent on Sunday
27 January 2013

In the most important foreign-policy speech of his premiership, David Cameron promised a referendum on Britain's membership of the European Union if the Conservatives won the next election.

Martin Rowson
The Guardian
28 January 2013

Many low-income families and disabled people would be forced to move or face more cuts when the new 'spare-bedroom tax' came into force in April.

Steve Bell
The Guardian
31 January 2013

This cartoon's design was based on the question proposed by the Scottish Government for the independence referendum in 2014: 'Do you agree that Scotland should be an independent country? Yes/No.' Scottish Nationalists besieged the *Guardian* with angry comments. A Glasgow-based human-rights lawyer, Aamer Anwar, for example, said it was 'derogatory and offensive'. It even led to an official quote from a *Guardian* spokeswoman to qualify the situation: 'It's a commentary on Alex Salmond's vision of an independent Scotland and reflects Bell's view [that] it would be against Scotland's interests.'

'I don't understand. Charles and Camilla said it was quite jolly.'

Mac
Daily Mail
31 January 2013

Camilla and Prince Charles travelled on a Metropolitan underground train from Farringdon to King's Cross to mark the 150th anniversary of the London Underground.

THE SIX NATIONS KICKS OFF

Patrick Blower
The Daily Telegraph
2 February 2013

Iran announced plans to install advanced uranium-enrichment machines that would allow them to significantly speed up the development of a nuclear weapon. As a consequence, Israel hinted at possible military action against Iran if sanctions and diplomacy failed to resolve the nuclear stand-off. In Egypt, protesters held a million-man march against the government, while civil unrest continued in Iraq, Mali, and Syria.

Paul Thomas
Daily Express
5 February 2013

A skeleton found beneath a Leicester car park was confirmed as that of Richard III. Experts from the University of Leicester said DNA from the bones matched that of descendants of the monarch's family. The bones had been subjected to 'rigorous academic study' and had been carbon dated to a period from 1455–1540. Richard was killed in battle in 1485.

Peter Brookes
The Times
6 February 2013

The government won a vote on gay marriage but more conservative MPs voted against it than supported the bill. David Cameron described the move as 'an important step forward' that strengthens society. Tory activists suggested Cameron's support for gay marriage has made winning the general election 'virtually impossible'.

Steve Bell
The Guardian
8 February 2013

The education secretary, Michael Gove, made a U-turn when he announced he was pulling back from plans to scrap GCSEs.

'He's right, you know — we've never had a Pope Tony.'

Mac
Daily Mail
12 February 2013

Pope Benedict XVI stepped down as pope at the age of 85. Ladbrokes placed Tony Blair at 500–1 to become the next pope.

Paul Thomas
Daily Express
13 February 2013

Pope Benedict XVI's decision to retire as leader of the Catholic Church made him the first pope to relinquish the office since Pope Gregory XII in 1415. The move was unexpected as popes have held the position from election until death. The pope stated that the reason for his decision was his declining health due to old age.

'Well, it says pork on the label.'

Mac
Daily Mail
15 February 2013

Waitrose announced it had withdrawn its beef Essential British frozen meatballs after horsemeat was found in two batches. David Cameron promised that anyone involved in passing off horsemeat as beef would face the full force of the law.

Peter Brookes
The Times
15 February 2013

In a bid to outflank David Cameron, Ed Miliband and Ed Balls claimed Labour would use next month's budget to bring back the 10p rate of income tax controversially scrapped by Gordon Brown in 2007. The clear rejection of Brown and Labour's past was a tactical move by Miliband to restore the public's trust in Labour on the economy.

Scott Clissold
Daily Sport
17 February 2013

Miliband said he would finance the re-introduction of the 10p tax rate by raising £2 billion with a mansion tax, a move that would save basic-rate taxpayers £100 a year: 'Let me tell you about one crucial choice we would make, which is different from this government. We would tax houses worth over £2 million. And we would use the money to cut taxes for working people.'

'One more question, m'lud — does a full house beat a royal flush?'

Mac
Daily Mail
22 February 2013

The ex-wife of Chris Huhne faced a retrial after a jury described by a judge as suffering 'absolutely fundamental deficits in understanding' failed to reach a verdict in her case. Mr Justice Sweeney said he had never seen a situation like it in 30 years, after being presented with a list of ten questions by the jury, following nearly 14 hours of deliberations. Mr Justice Sweeney gave the jury lengthy directions in a bid to answer their questions, but less than two hours later they said it was highly unlikely they would reach a verdict.

Christian Adams
The Daily Telegraph
24 February 2013

The UK lost its top AAA credit rating for the first time since 1978 on expectations that growth would 'remain sluggish over the next few years'. George Osborne said the decision was 'a stark reminder of the debt problems facing our country'. The Oscars had just been held in Hollywood on 21 February.

Andy Davey
The Sun
28 February 2013

British Gas risked fresh anger from consumer groups as it reported an 11 per cent increase in annual profits to over £600 million, aided by domestic price rises and more gas use after the long spell of cold weather. This was combined with Phil Bentley, the managing director of British Gas, formally announcing his decision to leave the company with a combined share, salary, and pension package worth more than £10 million.

Dave Brown
The Independent
5 March 2013

Contrary to his initial denials, Cardinal Keith O'Brien made a partial admission that his sexual behaviour did 'fall beneath the standards expected'. According to the cartoonist, the cardinal's use of his pulpit to launch vitriolic attacks on gay rights meant he could not avoid the charge of hypocrisy, in what might otherwise have simply been a matter of personal failings.

Bob Moran
The Daily Telegraph
8 March 2013

In the lead-up to George Osborne's budget, Cameron made a speech on the economy in which he stated (referring to Labour's attitude to borrowing) that there was no 'Magic Money Tree'. According to the cartoonist: 'I liked the idea that no one had bothered to explain this to George and he was building his whole budget plan on this tree existing.'

Scott Clissold
Daily Star
10 March 2013

Business Secretary Vince Cable warned that serious damage would be done to industry if only certain government departments were subject to spending cuts. In a *Guardian* interview at the Lib Dem spring conference, he questioned whether departments such as health and development should be protected.

Paul Thomas
Daily Express
12 March 2013

David Cameron came under fire from Totnes MP Sarah Wollaston for having a cabinet that looked 'far too posh, male, and white'. Dr Wollaston said the cabinet needed 'to look and sound more like modern Britain', and stressed there were plenty of talented women to choose from.

Andy Davey
The Sun
12 March 2013

Former cabinet minister Chris Huhne and his ex-wife Vicky Pryce were each jailed for eight months for perverting the course of justice. Huhne had admitted asking Pryce to take his speeding points to avoid losing his licence in 2003, and Pryce was convicted of having agreed to do so.

'I've just heard the first cuckoo of spring — he was hammering on the door to come in.'

Mac
Daily Mail
13 March 2013

March 2013 turned out to be the second-coldest March in Britain since 1910. As well as being very cold, March was also very snowy and joined 2006, 2001, 1995, 1987, 1979, 1970, and 1962 as years when March saw significant snowfall.

THE HOLY SEE

Ingram Pinn
The Financial Times
16 March 2013

As Pope Francis took over at the Vatican, he was faced by hard issues, including the sexual-abuse scandals that had undermined the moral authority of the Catholic Church in recent years.

Martin Rowson
The Guardian
18 March 2013

A Commons showdown was set up by David Cameron when he dramatically ended negotiations to find a way to implement the recommendations of the Leveson Inquiry into phone hacking. He had said using legislation would endanger press freedom and was 'unnecessary and undesirable'.

Andy Davey
The Sun
20 March 2013

Cabinet ministers were told by George Osborne to find an extra £2.5 billion of cuts from their departmental budgets. According to the cartoonist: 'Spending ministers (Cable, May, Hammond, etc.) make protesting noises but there seems no doubt that their piggy banks will be smashed for the small change, come Spending Review time.'

Morten Morland
The Times
21 March 2013

George Osborne scrapped a 6p rise in the price of beer before cutting the cost of a pint by 1p to give British drinkers a boost. Wine drinkers, however, were unhappy as Mr Osborne still demanded the price of an average bottle increase. Experts suggested that this was another budget blunder by the chancellor as the Tories fought to attract female voters, the majority of whom drank wine not beer.

CARTOONIST OF THE YEAR

Christian Adams
The Daily Telegraph
26 March 2013

Boris Johnson admitted that he would like to be prime minister: 'If the ball came loose from the back of the scrum, which it won't, it would be a great, great thing to have a crack at.' However, his hopes suffered a setback after he floundered through an interview with Eddie Mair on BBC television. The media described the embarrassing exchange as a 'car crash' and Johnson's worst-ever interview.

Andy Davey
The Sun
28 March 2013

The Home Secretary, Theresa May, lost her latest legal attempt to deport the radical Islamist cleric Abu Qatada back to Jordan, but vowed 'this is not the end of the road'. According to the cartoonist: 'I imagine the atmosphere inside the Home Office is not fragrant. I like to think government frustration is vented this way — with voodoo dolls, mojos, and chicken feet. Better than the dumb-ass patronising PR we get from them when they are on TV.'

Making an Omelette

Chris Duggan
The Times
30 March 2013

The president of Cyprus, Nicos Anastasiades, said that his country had no intention of quitting the eurozone, but it would need to make sacrifices to restore its debt-plagued economy. The Cypriot government negotiated a €13 billion bailout whereby Cypriot bank depositors have been forced to bear some of the cost of the rescue plan.

Ben Jennings
i
30 March 2013

Protests were held over Easter in regard to the Coalition's bedroom tax. Over 13,000 people came out to protest at 52 locations, demanding an end to the changes. The scheme will see people of a working age in social housing with a spare bedroom have their housing benefit reduced by £40–£80 a month.

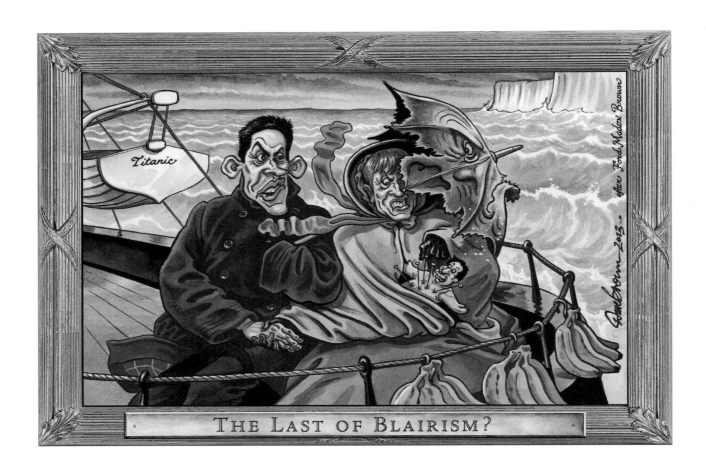

THE LAST OF BLAIRISM?

Dave Brown
The Independent
30 March 2013

David Miliband's decision to quit politics and become head of a charity based in New York was met with mixed reactions in Labour circles: relief for supporters of brother Ed, but dismay from 'Blairites' who still hoped he might eventually become leader. According to the cartoonist: 'In Ford Madox Brown's original painting, the stern of the ship the emigrants leave on is hung with cabbages. This was an attempt to keep them fresh on the long voyage, but provided me with the opportunity to replace them with that great comic symbol of Miliband's failure, bananas.'

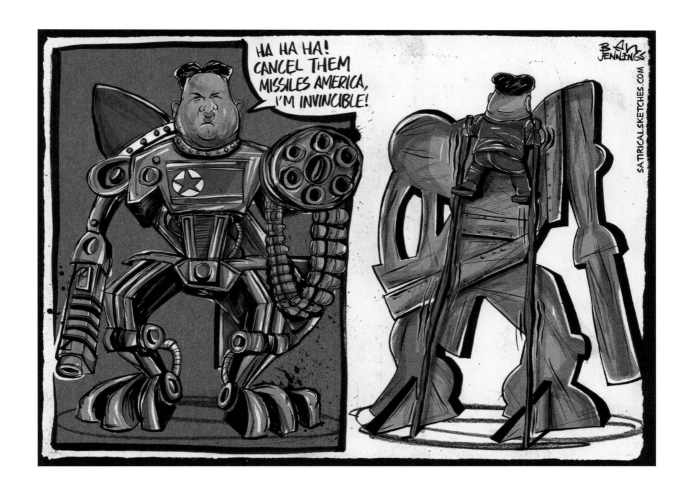

Ben Jennings
The Guardian
6 April 2013

Officials in Washington dismissed the threat of a nuclear strike against the United States as bluster by North Korea's leader, Kim Jong-un.

Chris Riddell
The Observer
7 April 2013

David Cameron warned that abandoning the Trident nuclear-defence capability would be 'foolish' in the face of the potential threat of nuclear attack from unstable states such as North Korea and Iran. Iain Duncan Smith had claimed he could live on £53 a week, the amount given to some benefit claimants. The Department for Work and Pensions secretary said he could survive on £7.57 per day if he 'had to', as he defended a raft of cuts to welfare payments.

Steve Bell
The Guardian
9 April 2013

Former prime minister Baroness Thatcher died aged 87 after suffering a stroke while staying at the Ritz hotel in central London. The *Daily Mail* criticised this cartoon for its 'vitriol' about her and said that it reflected 'poorly' on its author.

Morten Morland
The Times
15 April 2013

An online anti-Thatcher campaign failed to get the song 'Ding-Dong! The Witch Is Dead' to the top of the official UK singles chart. The recording, taken from the 1939 film *The Wizard of Oz*, entered the charts at number two. Some Tory MPs demanded the BBC ban the song, but others warned that politicians should not interfere in the choice of records played by broadcasters.

Peter Brookes
The Times
16 April 2013

A museum, library, and educational centre is being planned as a permanent memorial to Margaret Thatcher. Based on the Ronald Reagan Presidential Library, it aims to promote her political philosophy and shape future Conservative politics. The Conservative MP Conor Burns added: 'She believed in action and so along with the usual statues and portraits we thought it was vital to do something that will continue to actively contribute toward political debates long after her death.'

'I'm so glad you recorded this. I had my back to the funeral.'

Mac
Daily Mail
18 April 2013

Hundreds of protesters turned their backs on Margaret Thatcher's funeral procession as it passed through central London during a day of highly charged but peaceful demonstrations. Protest organisers had called for people to silently turn their back on Thatcher's coffin, but as it came into view there were shouts of 'What a waste of money' and 'Tory scum'. Similar shouts at other points on the route were drowned out by pro-Thatcher clapping.

THE GUN LOBBY...

US SENATE

19 iv 13
Peter Brookes

Peter Brookes
The Times
19 April 2013

A furious Barack Obama accused members of Congress of caving in to the gun lobby. Moderate Republicans and four Democrats bowed to pressure from the National Rifle Association and blocked a bipartisan senate amendment that would have expanded background checks for gun purchases to gun shows and online sales.

Bob Moran
The Daily Telegraph
19 April 2013

Nick Clegg insisted that MPs were not 'all Thatcherites now' as David Cameron had said in an attempt to be poignant. According to the cartoonist: 'Clegg is still desperately trying to be seen as a Liberal Democrat so he's dressed in his sandals and tank top and is refusing to put on the Maggie outfit like a grumpy teenager on a family trip.'

Ben Jennings
i
20 April 2013

Theresa May revealed that security would be tightened at the London Marathon in light of the bomb attacks at the finish line of the Boston Marathon the previous week. London police chiefs also sought to reassure people that the race would be safe.

Brighty
The Sun
22 April 2013

Sun correspondent Trevor Kavanagh suggested that the police were 'becoming a law unto themselves', more interested in prosecuting the press than traditional criminals: 'Last week, three civilians were arrested over stories that a police crime commissioner charged £700 for chauffeured cars despite being handed a new £23,000 Hyundai. You might think this information was in the public interest. No, they risk prison for misconduct in a public office in two cases and "perverting the course of justice" in one.'

Andy Davey
The Sun
23 April 2013

According to the cartoonist: 'Liverpool fined the humble, generous-hearted racist Luis Suárez for biting a Chelsea defender. Perhaps the dentist's mirror should be added to the referee's kit bag as a matter of course. Along with pepper spray and tasers.'

Paul Thomas
Daily Express
25 April 2013

Secret documents saved from a skip revealed *Winnie the Pooh* author A.A. Milne's confidential role as a World War I military-intelligence propagandist. The files showed his involvement with MI7b, a branch of MI7, designed to boost British wartime morale. It wrote positive newspaper stories and sanitised accounts of trench life.

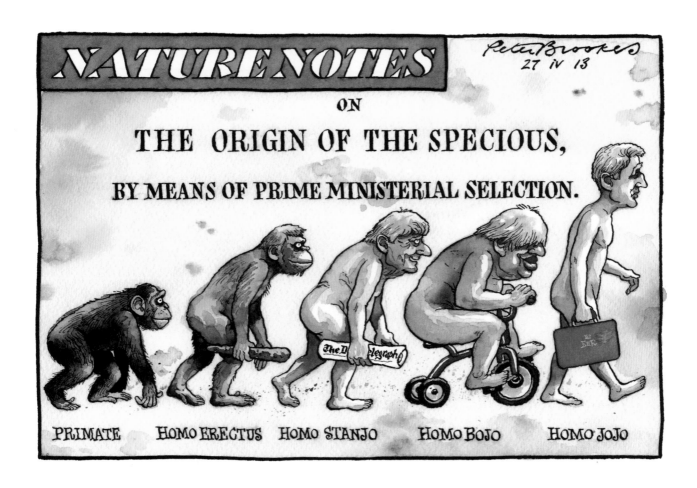

Peter Brookes
The Times
27 April 2013   Jo Johnson, the younger brother of Boris, was appointed head of David Cameron's policy unit at No. 10.

Chris Riddell
The Observer
28 April 2013

George Osborne was handed a rare encouraging assessment of the state of the economy as a survey of businesses predicted that Britain would avoid a triple-dip recession. The forecast from the British Chambers of Commerce suggested that the UK will not plunge into an unprecedented third downturn, but stated that any improvement in the economy is likely to be slow and protracted.

Peter Schrank
The Independent on Sunday
28 April 2013

President Obama had been calling for Syria's President Bashar al-Assad to surrender power for two years. Last year, he proclaimed a 'red line', a prohibition against the use of chemical weapons, and then watched as Assad crossed it.

Morten Morland
The Times
30 April 2013

On *The Andrew Marr Show*, David Cameron stated the need to 'get ourselves out of the mess that we were left by the last government'. While Cameron's popularity was shown to be at its lowest level since before the last election, a *Sunday Times* YouGov poll showed that only 17 per cent blamed the return to recession on the last Labour government.

Paul Thomas
Daily Express
2 May 2013

Stuart Hall's secret life as a serial sex offender was exposed as he admitted to 14 offences involving 13 victims dating back to the late 1960s, including an assault on a nine-year-old girl. Henry VIII was given a modern, digitally created makeover based on his portrait by Hans Holbein to tie in with the new historical TV series *The Secret Life of...*. Henry has retained his macho pose, but been put into a tailored Simon Cowell–type suit and an unbuttoned shirt, with a designer watch, very much the lady-killer (which Henry was, in more ways than one).

Bob Moran
The Daily Telegraph
4 May 2013

In the build-up to the local elections, David Cameron had called UKIP 'fruitcakes'. According to the cartoonist: 'Following UKIP's success, the obvious image was Farage bursting triumphantly from a giant fruitcake. Originally, he had no clothes on but, after some debate, I was persuaded to dress him.'

PRESIDENT AT BAY

Ingram Pinn
The Financial Times
4 May 2013

Controversy over the Guantánamo Bay detention camp intensified as United Nations experts condemned the force-feeding of hunger-striking inmates by the United States. Earlier, Barack Obama had vowed to make good on a broken promise, made during the 2008 presidential race, to get rid of the prison in Cuba.

Chris Riddell
The Observer
5 May 2013

Nigel Farage claimed UKIP was the country's third political force as the anti-EU party took chunks out of the Conservatives, Labour, and Lib Dems, grabbing 139 council seats. Farage, in a reference to Tory minister Kenneth Clarke's attack on his party as 'clowns' just days ago, declared: 'Send in the clowns.'

Peter Brookes
The Times
8 May 2013

Former Conservative chancellor Nigel Lawson dramatically called for Britain to leave the EU. Lawson described the EU as 'a bureaucratic monstrosity' and said the economic gains from leaving 'would substantially outweigh the costs'. Lawson pledged to vote No in a referendum on membership, a move that piled further pressure on David Cameron.

Scott Clissold
Daily Star
12 May 2013

Sir Alex Ferguson announced his retirement as the manager of Manchester United, ending the most successful managerial career in football. Ferguson admitted he pressured match officials into giving Manchester United what became known as 'Fergie time'.

'Chris has gone out. He asked me to wear his tag for him.'

Mac
Daily Mail
14 May 2013

Former cabinet minister Chris Huhne was released from Leyhill Prison in Gloucestershire after serving 62 days of an eight-month sentence for perverting the course of justice after asking his then wife, Vicky Pryce, to take three speeding points for him a decade ago. They were freed under home-detention curfew and forced to each wear an electronic tag.

Peter Brookes
The Times
15 May 2013

More than 100 Conservative MPs defied the government by backing an amendment to the Queen's speech on an EU referendum. They 'expressed regret' that a bill paving the way for a referendum in 2017, as pledged by David Cameron, was not being brought forward this year. The backers of the amendment included 116 Tory MPs, representing half of all the party's backbenchers.

Paul Thomas
Daily Express
17 May 2013

According to Stephen Pollard in the *Daily Express*, 'Seventy years after the Dambusters raid and 68 years after the end of the war we are now part of a project to unify Europe, a project for which none of us has ever voted and which all the evidence shows only a small minority support. Not just here but across the EU.'

The Once and Future King...

Chris Duggan
The Times
18 May 2013

Outgoing Bank of England governor Mervyn King warned that the bank could not be run as 'a one-man show' when his successor Mark Carney took over. He was concerned about expectations that the Canadian's arrival would lead to a quick fix for Britain's slow economy.

NIGEL IN SCOTLAND

Bob Moran
The Daily Telegraph
18 May 2013

Nigel Farage visited Scotland, where he received a lot of abuse from Scottish nationalists. According to the cartoonist: 'I decided to do snapshots of him doing typical things one might do in Scotland but not enjoying them. My editor is Scottish and this went down very well with him.'

Chris Riddell
The Observer
19 May 2013

David Cameron was struggling to maintain Tory discipline over Europe after cabinet loyalists Michael Gove and Philip Hammond said they would vote to leave the European Union if a referendum were to be held immediately. Gove confirmed for the first time that he believed that leaving the EU would have 'certain advantages'. The timing of this would have caused consternation for Cameron, as he was attending talks with Barack Obama in the White House, where he was pressing for an EU–US trade deal that he claimed would bring £10 billion of annual benefits to Britain.

Morten Morland
The Times
20 May 2013

According to the cartoonist, this cartoon relates to the perceived uselessness of the Coalition after yet more squabbles and policy cock-ups. Lord Ashcroft, a former Tory Party treasurer, called for an end to the the rows over Europe, gay marriage, and 'loongate'.

Brighty
The Sun
20 May 2013

Two newspapers revealed that a member of Cameron's inner circle had described grassroots Conservatives pushing for an EU referendum as 'mad, swivel-eyed loons'. In an attempt to limit the damage caused by the affair, he attempted to assure party members in an email that neither he nor his inner circle would ever 'sneer' at them. Cameron did not refer explicitly to the remark, but insisted that he admired and respected his party's activists. 'I am proud to lead this party. I am proud of what you do,' he said.

Patrick Blower
The Daily Telegraph
24 May 2013

A British Army soldier, Lee Rigby, was killed by two assailants near the Royal Artillery Barracks in Woolwich, south-east London, in what was described as a terrorist attack. Two men ran him down with a car, then used knives and a cleaver to stab and hack him to death.

Patrick Blower
The Daily Telegraph
25 May 2013

Forbes ranked German Chancellor Angela Merkel as the most powerful woman in the world. The Queen and J.K. Rowling were once again the only two British women to feature in the *Forbes* Most Powerful Women list, which was led by Angela Merkel for the third year running.

Scott Clissold
Daily Star
26 May 2013

Muslim leaders accused far-right extremists of trying to capitalise on the 'sick and barbaric' murder of Lee Rigby to fuel racial hatred. Islamophobic hate crimes were running at more than ten times their usual rate, with more than 140 reported to a government-backed hotline in the 48 hours after the Woolwich killing.

'Typical. It's the weekend, you're relaxing with friends in the pub, then some b*****d has to have an emergency operation.'

Mac
Daily Mail
30 May 2013

A *British Medical Journal* report into non-emergency operations in England suggested that people who have surgery towards the end of the week are more likely to die than those who have procedures earlier on.

Bob Moran
The Daily Telegraph
1 June 2013

President Vladimir Putin said that Russia would not rule out sending fresh arms to the Syrian regime and warned the West against arming 'criminals' in the rebellion: 'We are supplying arms to the legitimate government in accordance with legal contracts.'

Scott Clissold
Daily Star
2 June 2013

Patrick Mercer MP resigned from the Conservative parliamentary party for failing to declare thousands of pounds paid by a fake lobbying firm in a journalistic sting. David Cameron then came under pressure for failing to introduce promised legislation to expose the activities of lobbying companies. One Conservative source said: 'The PM wanted sleaze allegations to be a thing of the past but they are coming thick and fast now.'

Peter Schrank
*The Independent
on Sunday*
2 June 2013

Google faced calls to do more against child pornography after Mark Bridger was found guilty of murdering April Jones.
Labour called on search engines and other technology companies to be more 'proactive' in blocking access to child
pornography.

Peter Brookes
The Times
4 June 2013

Lords Cunningham, Mackenzie, and Laird were to be investigated by the House of Lords standards commissioner after they broke rules by offering to carry out parliamentary work for cash.

'We've timed you, sunshine. You've been hogging the centre lane for over an hour now!'

Mac
Daily Mail
5 June 2013

Motorway tailgaters and middle-lane hoggers now face quick justice with on-the-spot penalties under new measures announced by the government. As of July 2013, police have been able to issue £100 fines and three penalty points for careless driving offences that would have previously gone to court.

Steve Bell
The Guardian
7 June 2013

Work and pensions secretary Iain Duncan Smith described Labour's new plans for housing-benefit reform as 'vacuous' and 'more an excuse than a policy'. Nevertheless, the Conservatives were surprised that Miliband had, in effect, announced that he would accept all the Coalition's spending cuts unless Labour could find money from elsewhere (not from borrowing) to pay for them to be reversed.

THE BLIND LEADING THE BLIND IN IRAQ, AFGHANISTAN, LIBYA, SYRIA... *Peter Brookes* AFTER BRUEGEL

8 vi 13

Peter Brookes
The Times
8 June 2013

Cabinet ministers feared David Cameron was in danger of aping Tony Blair as the prime minister pushed for the arming of Syrian rebels and even held out the prospect of military intervention. As 81 Tory MPs signed a letter to No. 10 demanding a substantive Commons vote before arms were sent to the rebels, senior figures warned of parallels between Cameron and Blair as the tenth anniversary of the Iraq war was marked.

SNOOP

Blower
with acknowledgments 8·6·13

Patrick Blower
The Daily Telegraph
8 June 2013

Barack Obama struck a defiant tone amid revelations over the extent of surveillance operations by the United States federal government, arguing that the programs had full congressional approval while also criticising 'leaks' and 'hype' in the media. He did acknowledge, however, that authorities had undertaken a seven-year program to monitor the telephone calls of potentially millions of people in the United States.

Chris Riddell
The Observer
16 June 2013

Theresa May was widely perceived as positioning herself as a future leadership contender. In a wide-ranging speech seen as her putting down a marker for a future Tory leadership contest: 'We have to become the party that takes power from the elites and gives it to the people, the party not just of those who have already made it, but the home of those who want to work hard and get on in life.'

Steve Bell
The Guardian
18 June 2013

The Taliban and the United States agreed to hold talks on finding a political solution to ending nearly 12 years of war in Afghanistan.

Paul Thomas
Daily Express
19 June 2013

Leaders of the G8 group of world powers agreed to reach a joint position on Syria that could pave the way for new peace talks in Geneva. Police inquired into reports that the millionaire art collector Charles Saatchi gripped his wife, Nigella Lawson, by the throat several times during an argument outside a London restaurant. Photographs of the incident at Scott's restaurant in Mayfair appeared in the *Sunday People*.

POLICE MUGSHOTS

1960s

1980s

2010s

Andy Davey
The Sun
(unpublished)

A former undercover Metropolitan Police officer alleged he was told by his superiors to pose for four years as an anti-racist campaigner in order to find 'dirt' that could be used against members of the Stephen Lawrence family. The plan was to smear and undermine the family's campaign against racism in the police force. Doreen Lawrence's reaction said it all: 'Out of all the things I've found out over the years, this has certainly topped it.'

Chris Riddell
The Observer
9 June 2013

In order to attract middle-class support, Ed Miliband announced that, if in office, a new Labour government would cap the welfare budget. Miliband was also facing Conservative claims of 'hypocrisy' after it emerged that Labour had helped John Mills avoid tax of up to £1.5 million by accepting a £1.65 million donation in the form of shares in his JML shopping-channel company rather than in cash.

Steve Bell
The Guardian
20 June 2013

During a visit to Berlin, Barack Obama called for a major new push to reduce the world's nuclear arsenal, declaring that he would seek talks with Russia to reduce deployed nuclear weapons by up to one third. 'We intend to work with Russia to move beyond Cold War nuclear posturing,' he said.

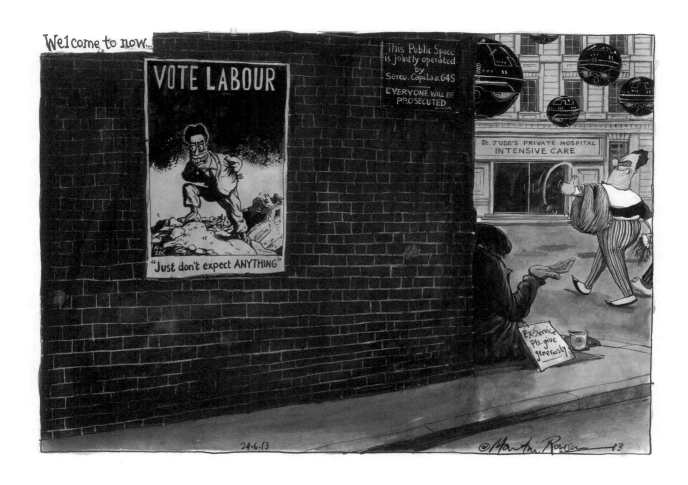

Martin Rowson
The Guardian
24 June 2013

Ed Miliband told party activists that Labour would not increase borrowing to reverse spending cuts as he warned the party must appear 'credible'. Miliband said Labour must face up to the 'hard reality' that it will not be able to reverse spending cuts scheduled by the coalition for 2015–16. 'When George Osborne stands up next week and announces his cuts we won't be able to promise now to reverse them because we've got to be absolutely crystal clear about where the money is coming from.'

Brighty
The Sun
8 July 2013

Ed Miliband pledged to end the automatic 'affiliation' fee paid by three million union members to Labour. This came about after the Unite union was accused of trying to rig the selection of Labour's parliamentary candidate for Falkirk. The Labour leader said changing its link with the unions would mean an end to 'machine politics' and prove that he was not in thrall to the union puppet masters. However, Unite general secretary Len McCluskey said the fee, worth £8 million a year to Labour, would 'stay as it is'.

Dave Brown
The Independent
8 July 2013

Abu Qatada was finally deported from Britain after a ten-year legal battle that cost the British taxpayers an estimated £2 million. Home Secretary Theresa May said that she was 'very pleased' to have finally succeeded in deporting the cleric. 'He is now where people want him to be — which is not in the UK, but back in Jordan,' she said.

Steve Bell
The Guardian
9 July 2013

After Andy Murray defeated world number one Novak Djokovic, David Cameron said that Murray deserved a knighthood for becoming the first Briton to win the Wimbledon men's singles since 1936. Scottish First Minister Alex Salmond was accused of staging a political stunt after smuggling the Scottish Saltire in his wife's handbag and waving it behind Cameron's head. Salmond insisted no one stuck to the rule banning large flags around Centre Court, and after waiting 117 years for a Scot to win the men's singles, 'a few Saltires hoisted over Wimbledon does not do any harm at all'.

Peter Brookes
The Times
11 July 2013

Tony Blair suggested that the Egyptian army was right to overthrow Islamist president Mohamed Morsi in order to prevent the country sliding into chaos. Blair, now a Middle East envoy, said that the international community must work with Egypt's new government to help it stabilise the country and work towards democratic elections.

Peter Brookes
The Times
16 July 2013

David Cameron was being pushed to do more to intervene in Syria's civil war by his wife, Samantha Cameron. She had called for a robust response to the humanitarian crisis in Syria after travelling to the region in her role as a charity envoy. 'With every day that passes, more children and parents are being killed, more innocent childhoods are being smashed to pieces,' she said.

Peter Brookes
The Times
17 July 2013

As further cuts to the number of NHS nurses were announced, the prime minister refused to discuss Lib Dem requests to cut the cost of Trident submarines, which could save tens of billions of pounds of taxpayers' money. A spokesman for David Cameron said he was 'crystal clear' that Britain needed a continuous at-sea deterrent at a time of 'evolving threats around nuclear proliferation'.

Peter Schrank

The Independent
on Sunday
18 July 2013

Heathrow airport officials put forward three options for a third runway at the west London site, saying any of the proposals would be good for Britain. Each option would let Heathrow move from 480,000 flights a year to 700,000 or more.

Patrick Blower
The Daily Telegraph
20 July 2013

Detroit, known as 'Motor City' for its once thriving motor-car industry, became the largest American city to file for bankruptcy, with debts of at least ten billion pounds. Public services are near to collapse and about 70,000 properties lie abandoned.

Chris Riddell
The Observer
21 July 2013   The House of Commons adjourned on 18 July for the summer recess and would not sit again until 2 September 2013.

Brighty
The Sun
21 July 2013

As the Duchess of Cambridge went into labour, bookmakers were inundated with bets on the soon-to-be-born royal baby. Betting agency Coral described it as the biggest non-sporting betting event in the company's history. 'The whole world has been waiting for Kate to go into labour and now that she has, we have witnessed another betting frenzy,' said a spokeswoman for the firm. The cartoonist seems to have received some inside information as he prophetically has George down as the most likely choice of boy's name.

Christian Adams
The Daily Telegraph
24 July 2013

The Duke and Duchess of Cambridge's new baby made royal history as it became the third living heir in waiting to the throne.

Chris Riddell
The Observer
28 July 2013

George Osborne's latest attempt to kickstart the economy by spending billions of pounds on underwriting a homebuying revival came under fire from economists and politicians, with one leading business body branding it 'very dangerous'. The Institute of Directors joined critics who claimed the scheme to partially guarantee more than 500,000 low-deposit mortgages over three years risked creating a new housing bubble.

Dave Brown
The Independent
30 July 2013

Israeli and Palestinian teams flew to Washington, DC, to end five years of diplomatic stalemate and prepare for a new round of peace talks, though optimism was in short supply after two decades of failed attempts to reach a settlement. Palestinian President Mahmoud Abbas has been reluctant to negotiate with Israeli Prime Minister Benjamin Netanyahu, fearing the hardline Israeli leader will reject what the Palestinians consider minimal territorial demands.

Gary Barker
The Times
31 July 2013

President Robert Mugabe vowed to step down if he lost the Zimbabwe general election. 'If you lose you must surrender,' the 89-year-old veteran said at a press conference in Harare on the eve of the vote. Mugabe, through a series of violent and suspect elections, has ruled Zimbabwe for 33 years. Mugabe denied any attempts to rig the election, declaring: 'We have done no cheating.'

HUNG OUT TO DRY...

Dave Brown
The Independent
1 August 2013

American soldier Bradley Manning was found guilty of espionage for leaking US government secrets. Manning, in full military uniform, showed little emotion during his nine-minute judgement that could see him jailed for 136 years for handing classified information to WikiLeaks, the anti-secrecy website headed by Julian Assange. Manning was working as an intelligence analyst near Baghdad when he was arrested more than three years ago, and he has been detained ever since.

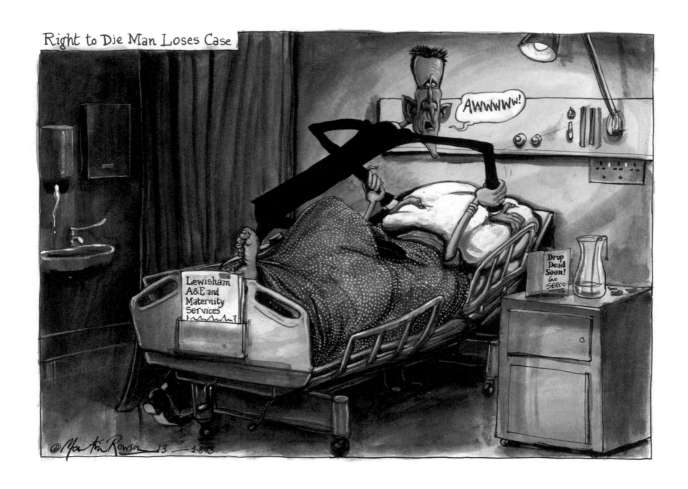

Martin Rowson
The Guardian
1 August 2013

Secretary of State for Health Jeremy Hunt's plan to reduce casualty and maternity services at Lewisham hospital was declared unlawful by the High Court. Mr Justice Silber said the secretary of state had breached provisions of the *National Health Services Act 2006*.

Dave Brown
The Independent
2 August 2013

Documents released from the National Archives revealed that Margaret Thatcher vetoed plans to give William Hague a job as a Treasury adviser to Geoffrey Howe in 1983. The then prime minister dismissed the plan to employ the 21-year-old, based on his famous speech to the Conservative party when he was 16, as a 'gimmick'. Giving him a job could prove an 'embarrassment', Mrs Thatcher had added.

Morten Morland
The Times
3 August 2013

Italy's supreme court upheld a jail sentence against Silvio Berlusconi for both tax fraud and for having had sex with a minor. Due to his age, he was ordered to serve the sentence under house arrest in only one of his many houses. In a sober video message after the verdict, Berlusconi proclaimed his total innocence and launched a bitter attack on the magistrates that, he said, had hounded him for 20 years and become an undemocratic rival power to the state.

Ben Jennings
The Independent
3 August 2013

The appointment of big donors from the three main political parties to the House of Lords was criticised as being 'indefensible' and 'out of touch'. The Liberal Democrat peer, Lord Oakeshott, said the list was 'polluting' parliament.

Peter Schrank

*The Independent
on Sunday*
4 August 2013

Twitter announced plans to introduce a 'report abuse' button following the abusive tweets, including rape and death threats, to historian Mary Beard, British feminist campaigner Caroline Criado-Perez, and the British MP Stella Creasy. Three men were arrested under the *Protection from Harassment Act 1997* in connection with the incidents.

Relations between Britain and Spain deteriorated as David Cameron admitted to being 'seriously concerned' over Spain's warning that it was considering imposing new controls relating to leaving or entering Gibraltar. A row over fishing in the sea near the Rock of Gibraltar — whose British sovereignty Spain disputes — sparked the latest tensions. In July, Gibraltar ordered massive blocks of concrete studded with hooks to be dropped into the water, preventing Spanish vessels from fishing there.

Peter Brookes
The Times
6 August 2013

Peter Schrank
The Independent on Sunday
11 August 2013

The UK advertising watchdog launched an investigation into the Home Office's highly controversial 'Go Home or Face Arrest' campaign after complaints that it could incite or exacerbate racial tensions. The campaign involved mobile vans driven through six London boroughs carrying billboards urging illegal immigrants to return home voluntarily.

Chris Riddell
The Observer
11 August 2013

UKIP MEP Godfrey Bloom was forced by his leader, Nigel Farage, to issue a public apology after saying Britain should not send foreign aid to 'bongo-bongo land'. In a statement, he said he regretted any offence or embarrassment caused by the remark but denied that his comments had been racist and declared: 'What's wrong with that? I'm not a wishy-washy Tory.'

Christian Adams
The Daily Telegraph
12 August 2013

Ed Miliband vowed not to be panicked into a knee-jerk response to disquiet in Labour ranks over its summer performance and the slow slide in the party's opinion-poll lead over the Conservatives. The Labour leader returned from a fortnight's holiday in France to growing complaints that the opposition had been virtually invisible in recent weeks, allowing the Coalition to set the agenda.

Morten Morland
The Times
12 August 2013

Twenty-six police officers were injured during loyalist protests in Belfast as demonstrations were held against a republican parade. Police said they came under heavy and sustained attack by crowds 'intent on creating disorder'.

Dave Brown
The Independent
13 August 2013

Shadow Immigration Minister Chris Bryant claimed that the supermarket giant Tesco had undercut the wages of its British employees by recruiting cheap labour from Eastern Europe.

Dave Brown
The Independent
15 August 2013

Egyptian security forces crushed the protest camps of thousands of supporters of the deposed Islamist president Mohamed Morsi, shooting approximately 600 of them dead.

Chris Riddell
The Observer
18 August 2013

The Egyptian army's continued killing of protesters deepened the divide between the Islamists led by the Muslim Brotherhood, and the secularists, liberals, moderate Muslims, and minority Christians.

Brighty
The Sun
19 August 2013

The Archbishop of Canterbury turned down an invitation to be a patron of the RSPCA. The archbishop's refusal of the position is his most recent break with tradition, with four of his predecessors having assumed the role in the past. Since taking office in March, he has made bureaucratic changes at Lambeth Palace and spoken out against the Church of England's association with money-making organisations such as Wonga, the payday loan company.

Christian Adams
The Daily Telegraph
19 August 2013

Critics dismissed claims that the SAS had murdered Princess Diana as a 'mystifying stunt' based on 'nonsense' evidence from an 'erratic' sniper, in jail for illegally keeping guns at home. August is officially the period of the summer that journalists have traditionally called the 'Silly Season'. Many stories such as this would normally be dismissed on a busy news day. A skit published by *The Sunday Times* in 1955 described the Silly Season as 'the month of strange reports in newspapers, supposedly put together by second-eleven journalists'.

Morten Morland
The Times
29 August 2013

Cameron and Obama moved closer to military intervention in Syria as they agreed that chemical-weapon attacks by the Assad regime had taken the crisis into a new phase that merited a 'serious response'. In May 2003, a banner proclaiming 'mission accomplished' on the aircraft carrier where President George W. Bush declared an end to major combat in Iraq later came back to haunt him as the war lasted another eight brutal years.